easy meals

Mexican

p

This is a Parragon Book
First printed in 2001

Parragon
Queen Street House
4 Queen Street
Bath BA1 1HE
United Kingdom

ISBN: 0-75255-765-3

Printed in Spain

Produced by The Bridgewater Book Company Ltd, Lewes, East Sussex

Creative Director Terry Jeavons
Art Director Sarah Howerd
Editorial Director Fiona Biggs
Senior Editor Mark Truman
Editorial Assistant Tom Kitch
Page Make-up Chris Akroyd

NOTES FOR THE READER

- This book uses both metric and imperial measurements. Follow the same units of measurement throughout; do not mix metric and imperial.
- All spoon measurements are level: teaspoons are assumed to be 5 ml, and table-spoons are assumed to be 15 ml.
- Unless otherwise stated, milk is assumed to be full-fat, eggs and individual vegetables such as potatoes are medium-sized, and pepper is freshly ground black pepper.
- Recipes using raw or very lightly cooked eggs should be avoided by infants, the elderly, pregnant women, convalescents, and anyone suffering from an illness.
- Optional ingredients, variations, and serving suggestions have not been included in the calculations.
- The times given are an approximate guide only. Preparation times differ according to the techniques used by different people, and the cooking times vary as a result of the type of oven used.

Contents

Introduction

Mexican cookery takes familiar, everyday ingredients – meat and poultry, fish, cheese and eggs – and presents them in a way that is new and very quick and easy to prepare and cook. The addition of a fiery chilli or two, a few garlic cloves and plenty of fresh coriander, chopped finely to release its distinctive flavour, transforms a simple dish into a taste sensation – and this is only the beginning. Peppers, tomatoes, a whole range of herbs and spices, beans, raisins and even chocolate find their way into the Mexican cooking pot. Creamy, pale green avocados are a favourite, in salads and as the base of guacamole, a chunky dip. Tortillas, a thin, delicious bread made from maize flour, are as versatile as pasta, rice or potatoes. They are served with almost everything, in a variety of ways: cut into triangles as an accompaniment or a garnish, layered with a meat mixture, topped with cheese and baked, folded or rolled round a filling.

guide to recipe key	
easy	Recipes are graded as follows: 1 pea = easy; 2 peas = very easy; 3 peas = extremely easy.
serves 4	Recipes generally serve four people. Simply halve the ingredients to serve two, taking care not to mix imperial and metric measurements.
15 minutes	Preparation time. Where recipes include marinating, soaking, standing, or chilling, these times are listed separately: eg, 15 minutes, plus 30 minutes to marinate.
15 minutes	Cooking time. Cooking times do not include the cooking of rice or noodles to be served with the main dishes.

Mexican cooking is great fun for informal parties. The enticing names of the dishes make a good talking point as they roll lazily off the tongue – pozole, quesadillas, enchiladas, chilaquiles, burritos, fajitas, nachos. Some recipes are intended for self-assembly by guests, because to serve a pot of sizzling hot spicy meat, a plate of crisp raw vegetables, some cool, soured cream and a stack of warm tortillas, and invite everyone to create their own meal, is a marvellous ice-breaker. Add one or two colourful salsas and be prepared to shed many of your inhibitions about food and eating when you experiment with Mexican cooking.

Classic Beef Fajitas, page 36

Soups & Starters

Mexican soups and starters can make a stylish start to a meal. If you think of soups as light and bland, the Yucatan Citrus Soup, combining the kick of garlic and chillies with the refreshing tang of citrus rind and juice, may change your mind. The tangy flavour of Authentic Guacamole will challenge your preconceptions, as well as your taste buds, and for a starter to linger and chat over, serve Chorizo Artichoke Heart Quesadillas, a heart-warming dish of warm tortillas topped with meat and melting, bubbling cheese. And for hot days there is an Iced Salsa Soup.

Mexican-style Beef & Rice Soup

INGREDIENTS

3 tbsp olive oil
500 g/1 lb 2 oz boneless
   stewing beef, cut into
   2.5 cm/1 inch/pieces
150 ml/5 fl oz red wine
1 onion, chopped finely
1 green pepper, cored,
   deseeded and
   chopped finely
1 small fresh red chilli,
   deseeded and
   chopped finely
2 garlic cloves, chopped
   finely
1 carrot, chopped finely
¼ tsp ground coriander
¼ tsp ground cumin
⅛ tsp ground cinnamon
¼ tsp dried oregano
1 bay leaf
grated rind of ½ orange
400 g/14 oz canned
   chopped tomatoes
5 cups beef stock
50 g/1¾oz long-grain
   white rice
3 tbsp raisins
15 g/½ oz plain
   chocolate, melted
chopped fresh
   coriander, to garnish

❶ Heat half the oil in a large frying pan over a medium–high heat. Add the meat in one layer and cook until well browned, turning to colour all sides. Remove the pan from the heat and pour in the wine.

❷ Heat the remaining oil in a large saucepan over a medium heat. Add the onion, then cover and cook for about 3 minutes, stirring occasionally, until just softened. Add the green pepper, chilli, garlic and carrot, and continue cooking, covered, for 3 minutes.

❸ Add the coriander, cumin, cinnamon, oregano, bay leaf and orange rind. Stir in the tomatoes and stock, along with the beef and wine. Bring almost to the boil and when the mixture begins to bubble, reduce the heat to low. Cover and simmer gently, stirring occasionally, for about 1 hour, or until the meat is tender.

❹ Stir in the rice, raisins and chocolate, and continue cooking, stirring occasionally, for about 30 minutes, or until the rice is tender.

❺ Ladle into warm bowls and garnish with coriander.

 very easy

 serves 4

 15 minutes

 2 hours

 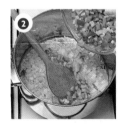 

Piquant Oatmeal Soup

INGREDIENTS

75 g/3 oz rolled oats
40 g/1½ oz butter
1 large sweet onion,
    chopped finely
2–3 garlic cloves
350 g/12 oz tomatoes,
    skinned, deseeded,
    and chopped
1.5 litres/2½ pints
    chicken stock
⅛ tsp ground cumin
1 tsp harissa, or ½ tsp
    chilli paste
1–2 tbsp lime juice
salt and pepper
chopped spring onions,
    to garnish

 very easy

 serves 4

 10 minutes

45 minutes

COOK'S TIP
This soup is very quick to prepare once the oats are toasted. The oats could be prepared in advance at a convenient time.

❶ Place a heavy-based frying pan over a medium heat. Add the oats and toast for about 25 minutes, stirring frequently, until lightly and evenly browned. Remove the oats from the pan and allow to cool.

❷ Heat the butter in a large saucepan over a medium heat. Add the onion and garlic, and cook until the onion is softened.

❸ Add the tomatoes, stock, cumin, harissa or chilli paste, and a good pinch of salt to the softened onion and garlic.

❹ Stir in the oats and bring to the boil. Regulate the heat so that the soup boils gently, and cook for 6 minutes.

❺ Stir in 1 tablespoon of the lime juice. Taste and adjust the seasoning. Add more lime juice if desired. Ladle the soup into warm bowls and sprinkle with spring onions, to garnish, before serving.

Iced Salsa Soup

INGREDIENTS

2 large ears of corn, or
   225 g/8 oz frozen
   sweetcorn kernels
1 tbsp olive oil
1 orange or red pepper,
   cored, deseeded and
   chopped finely
1 green pepper, cored,
   deseeded and
   chopped finely
1 sweet onion, such as
   Vidalia, chopped
   finely
3 ripe tomatoes,
   skinned, deseeded,
   and chopped
½ tsp chilli powder, or
   to taste
125 ml/4 fl oz water
450 ml/16 fl oz tomato
   juice
chilli paste (optional)
salt and pepper

TO GARNISH
3–4 spring onions,
   chopped finely
coriander

❶ Cut the corn kernels from the cobs, or if using frozen sweetcorn, defrost, then drain.

❷ Heat the oil in a saucepan over a medium–high heat. Add the peppers and cook, stirring briskly, for 3 minutes. Add the onion and continue cooking for about 2 minutes, or until it starts to colour slightly.

❸ Add the tomatoes, sweetcorn and chilli powder. Continue cooking, stirring frequently, for 1 minute. Pour in the water and when it bubbles, reduce the heat, cover, and cook for an additional 4–5 minutes, or until the peppers are just barely tender.

❹ Transfer the mixture to a large container and stir in the tomato juice. Season with salt and pepper and add more chilli powder if desired. Cover and refrigerate until cold.

❺ Taste and adjust the seasoning. For a more spicy soup, stir in a little chilli paste to taste. For a thinner soup, add a small amount of iced water. Ladle into chilled bowls and garnish with spring onions and coriander.

 very easy

 serves 4

15 minutes, plus
4 hours to chill

 15 minutes

Yucatecan Citrus Soup

INGREDIENTS

2 onions
15 large garlic cloves,
    unpeeled
1 tbsp olive oil
1.5 litres/2½ pints
    vegetable, chicken or
    fish stock
250 ml/9 fl oz water
8 ripe tomatoes, diced
pinch of dried oregano
1 fresh green chilli, such
    as jalapeño or
    serrano, deseeded
    and chopped
pinch of ground cumin
½ tsp finely grated
    grapefruit rind
½ tsp finely grated lime
    rind
½ tsp finely grated
    orange rind
juice and diced flesh of
    2 limes
juice of 1 orange
juice of 1 grapefruit
salt and pepper

TO GARNISH
tortilla chips, or sliced
    tortilla strips fried
    until crisp
2 tbsp chopped fresh
    coriander

easy

serves 4–6

15 minutes

1 hour

❶ Cut one onion in half without peeling. Peel and finely chop the second onion.

❷ Heat a large heavy-based frying pan, add the unpeeled onion halves and garlic, then cook over a medium-high heat until the skins char and the onions are caramelized on their cut sides; the garlic should be soft on the inside. Remove the onion and garlic from the pan and set aside until cool enough to handle.

❸ Meanwhile, heat the oil in a pan and lightly sauté the remaining onion until it is softened. Add the stock and water and bring to the boil. Reduce the heat and simmer for a few minutes.

❹ Peel the charred onion and garlic, then chop roughly and add to the simmering soup, together with the tomatoes, chilli, oregano and cumin. Cook for about 15 minutes, stirring occasionally.

❺ Add the citrus rind, season with salt and pepper, then simmer for another 2 minutes. Remove from the heat and stir in the lime flesh and citrus juices.

❻ Ladle into soup bowls, garnish with tortilla chips and fresh coriander, then serve immediately.

Pozole

INGREDIENTS

450 g/1 lb pork for
    stewing, such as lean
    belly
½ small chicken
about 2 litres/3½ pints
    water
1 chicken stock cube
1 whole garlic bulb,
    divided into cloves but
    not peeled
1 onion, chopped
2 bay leaves
1 lb cooked hominy
¼–½ tsp ground cumin
salt and pepper

TO SERVE
½ small to medium
    cabbage, thinly sliced
dried oregano leaves
dried chilli flakes
tortilla chips
lime wedges

❶ Place the pork and chicken in a large pan. Add enough water to fill the pan. (Do not worry about having too much stock. It keeps fresh up to a week and freezes well.)

❷ Bring to the boil, then skim off the fat that rises to the surface. Reduce the heat and add the stock cube, garlic, onion and bay leaves. Simmer, covered, over a medium–low heat until the pork and chicken are tender and cooked through completely.

❸ Remove the pork and chicken from the soup and leave them to cool. When cool enough to handle, remove the chicken flesh from the bones and cut the pork into bite-sized pieces. Set aside.

❹ Skim the fat off the soup and discard the bay leaves. Add the hominy and cumin, salt and pepper, to taste. Bring to the boil.

❺ To serve, place a little pork and chicken in soup bowls. Top with cabbage, oregano and chilli flakes, then spoon in the hot soup. Serve with tortilla chips and lime.

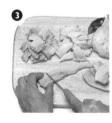

 very easy

 serves 4–6

 15 minutes

 1 hour

Authentic Guacamole

INGREDIENTS

1 ripe tomato
2 limes
2–3 ripe small to
    medium avocados, or
    1–2 large ones
$\frac{1}{4}$–$\frac{1}{2}$ onion, finely
    chopped
pinch of ground cumin
pinch of mild chilli
    powder
$\frac{1}{2}$–1 fresh green chillies,
    such as jalapeño or
    serrano, deseeded
    and finely chopped
1 tbsp finely chopped
    fresh coriander
    leaves, plus extra for
    garnishing
salt (optional)
tortilla chips, to serve
    (optional)

extremely easy

serves 4–6

10 minutes

0 minutes

❶ To skin the tomato, place in a heatproof bowl, then pour boiling water over to cover it and stand for 30 seconds. Drain and plunge into cold water. The skin will then slide off easily. Cut in half, deseed, and chop the flesh.

❷ Squeeze the juice from the limes into a bowl. Cut each avocado in half around the stone. Twist apart, then remove the stone with a knife. Carefully peel off the skin, dice the flesh, and toss in the bowl of lime juice to prevent discoloration. Repeat with the remaining avocados. Mash the avocados roughly.

❸ Add the onion, tomato, cumin, chilli powder, chillies and fresh coriander to the avocados. If using as a dip for tortilla chips, do not add salt. If using as a sauce, add salt to taste.

❹ To serve as a dip, transfer to a serving dish, then garnish with coriander and serve with tortilla chips.

COOK'S TIP

Avocados grow in abundance in Mexico, and Guacamole is used to add richness and flavour to all manner of dishes. Try spooning it into soups, especially those with chicken or seafood.

Salpicón of Crab

INGREDIENTS

¼ red onion, chopped
½–1 fresh green chilli,
    deseeded and
    chopped
juice of ½ lime
1 tbsp cider or other
    fruit vinegar, such as
    raspberry
1 tbsp chopped fresh
    coriander
1 tbsp extra-virgin olive
    oil
225–350 g/8–12 oz
    fresh crab meat
lettuce leave, to serve

TO GARNISH
1 avocado
lime juice, for tossing
1–2 ripe tomatoes
3-5 radishes

 extremely easy

 serves 4

 15 minutes

 0 minutes

VARIATION
Split open a long roll or
a bauette and heap
salpicón salad inside.
Top with a generous
layer of cheese, then
place the open roll
under the grill and
toast to melt the
cheese. Serve with
salsa.

❶ Combine the onion with the chilli, lime juice, vinegar, fresh coriander and olive oil. Add the crab meat and toss lightly together.

❷ To make the garnish, cut each avocado in half around the stone. Twist apart, then remove the stone with a knife. Carefully peel off the skin and slice the flesh. Toss gently in lime juice to prevent discoloration.

❸ Halve the tomatoes, then remove the cores and seeds. Dice the flesh. Slice the radishes thinly.

❹ Arrange the crab salad on a bed of lettuce leaves, then garnish with the avocado, tomatoes and radishes. Serve the salad at once.

Chorizo & Artichoke Heart Quesadillas

INGREDIENTS

1 chorizo sausage
1 large mild green chilli
   or green pepper
   (optional)
8–10 marinated artichoke
   hearts or canned arti-
   choke hearts, drained
   and diced
4 soft corn tortillas,
   warmed
2 garlic cloves, chopped
   finely
350 g/12 oz grated cheese
1 tomato, diced
2 spring onions, sliced
   thinly
1 tbsp chopped fresh
   coriander

❶ Dice the chorizo sausage. Heat a heavy-based frying pan, add the chorizo, and fry until it browns in places.

❷ If using the mild chilli or pepper, place under a preheated hot grill and grill for about 10 minutes, or until the skins are charred and the flesh softened. Place in a plastic bag and twist to seal, then set aside for 20 minutes. Remove the skins with a knife, then deseed and chop.

❸ Arrange the browned chorizo and artichoke hearts on the corn tortillas, then transfer half to a baking sheet.

❹ Sprinkle with the garlic, then the cheese. Place under a preheated hot grill, and grill until the cheese melts and sizzles. Repeat with the remaining tortillas.

❺ Sprinkle with the diced tomato, spring onions, green chilli or pepper (if using, and fresh coriander. Cut into wedges and serve.

 very easy

 serves 4

10 minutes,
plus 20 minutes
to stand

10 minutes

Meat

Mexican meat dishes are robust and rich. Many combine beef, pork, lamb, chicken or sausage with beans or a generous quantity of cheese. For a lighter variation on this theme, try the Steak, Avocado & Bean Salad, topped with a mildly spiced lime and olive oil dressing and garnished with crisp tortilla chips. Meatballs in Spicy-Sweet Sauce transforms ground meat by cooking it with colourful diced sweet potatoes, and serving it with grated cheese. Santa Fe Red Chilli Enchiladas uses tortillas imaginatively by stacking them in layers, interspersed with a filling of chilli and chicken, and topping each stack with a fried egg.

Steak, Avocado & Bean Salad

INGREDIENTS

350 g/12 oz tender steak, such as sirloin
4 garlic cloves, chopped
juice of 1 lime
4 tbsp extra-virgin olive oil
1 tbsp white or red wine vinegar
$\frac{1}{4}$ tsp mild chilli powder
$\frac{1}{4}$ tsp ground cumin
$\frac{1}{2}$ tsp paprika
pinch of sugar (optional)
5 spring onions, thinly sliced
about 200 g/7 oz crisp lettuce leaves, such as romaine
400 g/14 oz canned pinto, black or red kidney beans
1 avocado, stoned, sliced and tossed with a little lime juice
2 ripe tomatoes, diced
$\frac{1}{4}$ fresh green or red chilli, chopped
3 tbsp chopped fresh coriander
225 g/8 oz canned sweetcorn, drained
handful of tortilla chips, broken into pieces

 very easy

 serves 4

 10 minutes

 5–10 minutes

❶ Place the steak in a nonmetal dish with the garlic and half the lime juice and olive oil. Season with salt and pepper, then leave to marinate while you prepare the other ingredients.

❷ To make the dressing, combine the remaining lime juice and olive oil with the vinegar, chilli powder, cumin, and paprika. Add a pinch of sugar to taste. Set aside.

❸ Pan-fry the steak, or cook under a preheated grill, until browned on the outside and cooked to your liking in the middle. Remove from the pan, cut into strips, and reserve: keep warm or allow to cool.

❹ Toss the spring onions with the lettuce and arrange on a serving plate. Pour about half the dressing over the leaves, then arrange the beans, avocado and tomatoes over the top. Sprinkle with the chilli, coriander and sweetcorn.

❺ Arrange the steak and the tortilla chips on top, then pour the rest of the dressing over them. Serve immediately.

Santa Fe Red Chilli Enchiladas

INGREDIENTS

2–3 tbsp masa harina or
  1 corn tortilla,
  crushed or crumbled
4 tbsp mild chilli
  powder, such as New
  Mexico
2 tbsp paprika
2 garlic cloves, chopped
  finely
¼ tsp ground cumin
pinch of ground
  cinnamon
pinch of ground allspice
pinch of dried oregano
4 cups vegetable,
  chicken or beef stock,
  simmering
1 tbsp lime juice
1–2 tbsp extra-virgin
  olive oil
12 flour tortillas
about 450 g/1 lb cooked
  chicken or pork, cut
  into pieces
85 g/3 oz grated cheese
4–6 eggs

TO SERVE
½ onion, chopped finely
1 tbsp chopped finely
  fresh coriander
salsa of your choice

❶ Mix the masa harina with the chilli powder, paprika, garlic, cumin, cinnamon, allspice, oregano and enough water to make a thin paste. Process in a blender or a food processor until smooth.

❷ Stir the paste into the simmering stock, then reduce the heat and cook until it thickens slightly. Remove the sauce from the heat and stir in the lime juice.

❸ Dip the tortillas into the warm sauce. Cover one tortilla with cooked meat. Top with a second dipped tortilla, and cover with more meat, making a stack. Make 1–2 more stacks in this way, then transfer them to an ovenproof dish.

❹ Pour the remaining sauce over the tortillas, then sprinkle with the grated cheese. Bake in a preheated oven at 180°C/350°F/Gas Mark 4 for 15–20 minutes, or until the cheese has melted.

❺ Meanwhile, heat the olive oil in a nonstick frying pan. Fry the eggs until the whites are set but the yolks still soft.

❻ Serve cut into wedges and topped with an egg. Serve with the onion, coriander and salsa.

very easy

serves 4–6

10 minutes

20–25 minutes

Casserole of Tortilla Chips & Chorizo

12 stale tortillas, cut into strips
1 tbsp vegetable oil
2–3 chorizo sausages, sliced thinly or diced
2 garlic cloves, chopped finely
225 g/8 oz chopped canned tomatoes
3 tbsp chopped fresh coriander
2 cups chicken or vegetable stock
2 cups grated cheese
1 onion, chopped finely
salt and pepper

❶ Place the tortilla strips in a roasting tin and toss with the oil, then bake in a preheated oven at 190°C/375°F/Gas Mark 5 for about 30 minutes, or until they are crisp and golden.

❷ Brown the chorizo with the garlic in a frying pan until the meat is cooked. Pour away any excess fat, then add the tomatoes and the coriander to the pan and season with salt and pepper to taste. Set aside.

❸ In an ovenproof dish, about 30 cm/12 inches square, layer the tortilla chips and chorizo mixture, finishing with the tortilla chips.

❹ Pour the stock over the top of the dish, then sprinkle with the cheese. Bake in a preheated oven at 190°C/375°F/Gas Mark 5 for about 40 minutes, or until the cheese has melted and the tortilla chips are fairly soft.

❺ Serve immediately, sprinkled with the chopped onion.

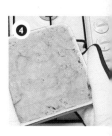

 extremely easy

 serves 4

 10 minutes

 1 hour, 20 minutes

Chicken Chilaquiles

12 stale tortillas, cut
    into strips
1 tbsp vegetable oil
1 small cooked chicken,
    meat removed from
    the bones and cut
    into bite-sized pieces
Salsa Verde
8 tbsp chopped fresh
    coriander
1 tsp finely chopped
    fresh oregano
    or thyme
4 garlic cloves, chopped
    finely
¼ tsp ground cumin
12 oz/350 g grated
    cheese, such as
    Cheddar, Manchego
    or mozzarella
2 cups chicken stock
125 g/4½ oz freshly
    grated Parmesan
    cheese

TO SERVE
1½ cups crème fraîche
    or soured cream
3–5 spring onions,
    sliced thinly
pickled chillies

❶ Place the tortilla strips in a roasting tin and toss with the oil, then bake in a preheated oven at 190°C/375°F/Gas Mark 5 for about 30 minutes, or until they are crisp and golden.

❷ Arrange the chicken in a 23 x 33 cm/9 x 13 inch casserole, then sprinkle with half the salsa verde, coriander, oregano, garlic, cumin and cheese. Repeat these layers and top with the tortilla strips.

❸ Pour the stock over the top, then sprinkle with the remaining cheeses.

❹ Bake in a preheated oven at 190°C/375°F/Gas Mark 5 for about 30 minutes, or until the cheese is lightly golden in areas.

❺ Garnish with the crème fraîche, spring onions, and pickled chillies to taste. Serve at once.

 extremely easy

 serves 4

 15 minutes

 1 hour

Burritos of Lamb & Black Beans

600 g/1 lb 5 oz lean
   lamb
3 garlic cloves, chopped
   finely
juice of ½ a lime
½ tsp mild chilli powder
½ tsp ground cumin
large pinch of dried
   oregano leaves,
   crushed
1–2 tbsp extra-virgin
   olive oil
400 g/14 oz cooked
   black beans,
   seasoned with a little
   cumin, salt and
   pepper
4 large flour tortillas
2–3 tbsp chopped fresh
   coriander
salsa, preferably
   Chipotle Salsa
salt and pepper

❶ Slice the lamb into thin strips, then combine with the garlic, lime juice, chilli powder, cumin, oregano and olive oil. Season with salt and pepper. Marinate in the refrigerator for 4 hours.

❷ Warm the black beans with a little water in a pan.

❸ Heat the tortillas in an ungreased nonstick frying pan, sprinkling them with a few drops of water as they warm; wrap the hot tortillas in a clean kitchen cloth to keep them warm. Alternatively, heat stack them in the pan and heat the stack through, alternating the top and bottom tortillas so that they warm evenly. Wrap them to keep them warm.

❹ Stir-fry the lamb in a heavy-based nonstick frying pan over a high heat until browned on all sides. Remove from the heat.

❺ Spoon some of the beans and browned meat into a tortilla, sprinkle with coriander, then dab with salsa and rol up. Repeat with the remaining tortillas and serve at once.

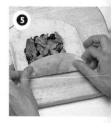

 extremely easy

 serves 4

 15 minutes,
plus 4 hours
to marinate

 20 minutes

Classic Beef Fajitas

700 g/1 lb 9 oz beef skirt
  steak or other tender
  steak, cut into strips
6 garlic cloves, chopped
juice of 1 lime
large pinch of mild chilli
  powder
large pinch of paprika
large pinch of ground
  cumin
1–2 tbsp extra-virgin
  olive oil
12 flour tortillas
vegetable oil, for frying
1–2 avocados, stoned,
  sliced and tossed
  with lime juice
½ cup soured cream
salt and pepper

PICO DE GALLO SALSA
8 ripe tomatoes, diced
3 spring onions, thinly
  sliced
1–2 fresh green chillies,
  such as jalapeño or
  serrano, deseeded
  and chopped
3–4 tbsp chopped fresh
  coriander
5–8 radishes, diced
ground cumin

❶ Combine the beef with half the garlic, half the lime juice, the chilli powder, paprika, cumin and olive oil. Add salt and pepper, mix well, and leave to marinate for at least 30 minutes at room temperature, or up to overnight in the refrigerator.

❷ To make the pico de gallo salsa, put the tomatoes in a bowl with the spring onions, green chilli, coriander and radishes. Season to taste with cumin, salt and pepper. Set aside.

❸ Heat the tortillas in a lightly greased nonstick frying pan, wrap in foil as you work, to keep them warm.

❹ Stir-fry the meat in a little oil over a high heat until browned and just cooked through.

❺ Serve the sizzling hot meat with the warm tortillas, the pico de gallo salsa, avocado and soured cream for each person to make his or her own rolled-up fajitas.

 extremely easy

 serves 4–6

 20 minutes,
plus 30 minutes
to marinate

 10–15 minutes

Michoacan Beef

INGREDIENTS

about 3 tbsp plain flour
1 kg/2 lb 4 oz stewing
*   beef, cut into large*
*   bite-sized pieces*
2 tbsp vegetable oil
2 onions, chopped
5 garlic cloves, chopped
400 g/14 oz tomatoes,
*   diced*
1½ dried chipotle
*   chillies,*
*   reconstituted,*
*   deseeded and cut*
*   into thin strips, or a*
*   few shakes of bottled*
*   chipotle salsa*
1.4 litres/2½ pints beef
*   stock*
350 g/12 oz French beans,
*   topped and tailed*
a pinch of sugar
salt and pepper

TO SERVE
simmered beans
cooked rice

❶ Place the flour in a large bowl and season with salt and pepper. Add the beef and toss to coat well. Remove from the bowl, shaking off the excess flour.

❷ Heat the oil in a frying pan and brown the meat briefly over a high heat. Reduce the heat to medium, then add the onions and garlic and cook for a further 2 minutes.

❸ Add the tomatoes, chillies and stock, then cover and simmer over a low heat for 1½ hours, or until the meat is very tender, adding the green beans 15 minutes before the end of the cooking time. Skim off any fat that rises to the surface.

❹ Transfer to individual bowls and serve with beans and rice.

 extremely easy

 serves 4

 15 minutes

 1 hour,
40 minutes

Meatballs in Spicy-sweet Sauce

INGREDIENTS

225 g/8 oz minced pork
225 g/8 oz minced beef
    or lamb
6 tbsp cooked rice or finely
    crushed tortilla chips
1 egg, lightly beaten
1½ onions, chopped
5 garlic cloves, chopped
½ tsp ground cumin
large pinch of ground
    cinnamon
2 tbsp raisins
1 tbsp dark brown sugar
1–2 tbsp cider or wine
    vinegar
400 g/14 oz canned
    tomatoes, drained
    and chopped
350 ml/12 fl oz beef
    stock
1–2 tbsp mild chilli or
    ancho chilli powder
1 tbsp paprika
1 tbsp chopped fresh
    coriander
1 tbsp chopped fresh
    parsley or mint
2 tbsp vegetable oil
2 sweet potatoes, peeled
    and cut into small bite-
    sized chunks
salt and pepper
grated cheese, to serve

 very easy

 serves 4

 15 minutes

45 minutes

❶ Mix the meat with the rice or crushed tortilla chips, the egg, half the onion, half the garlic, the cumin, cinnamon and raisins.

❷ Divide the mixture into even-sized pieces and roll into balls. Fry the balls in a nonstick frying pan over a medium heat, adding a tiny bit of oil, if necessary, to help them brown. Remove from the pan and set aside.

❸ Place the brown sugar in a blender or a food processor, with the vinegar, tomatoes, stock, chilli powder, paprika, and remaining onion and garlic. Process, then stir in the chopped fresh herbs. Set aside.

❹ Heat the oil in the cleaned frying pan, then add the sweet potatoes and cook until tender and golden. Pour in the blended sauce and add the meatballs. Cook for about 10 minutes, or until the meatballs are heated through and the flavours have combined. Season with salt and pepper. Serve accompanied by grated cheese.

Spicy Meat & Chipotle Hash

INGREDIENTS

1 onion, chopped finely
1 tbsp vegetable oil
450 g/1 lb leftover meat,
    eg simmered pork or
    beef, cooled and cut
    into thin strips
1 tbsp mild chilli powder
2 ripe tomatoes, diced
250 ml/9 fl oz meat stock
½–1 canned chipotle
    chillies, mashed, plus
    a little of the
    marinade
½ cup soured cream
4–6 tbsp chopped fresh
    coriander
4–6 tbsp chopped
    radishes
3–4 leaves crisp lettuce,
    such as romaine,
    shredded
12 flour tortillas, to
    serve

 very easy

 serves 4

 10 minutes

⊕ 30 minutes

COOK'S TIP
Avocados add an
interesting texture
contrast to the
spicy meat – serve with
2 sliced avocados,
tossed with lime juice.
Try serving on top of
crisply fried tortillas.

❶ Heat the oil in a frying pan, then add the onion and cook until softened, stirring occasionally. Add the meat and sauté for about 3 minutes, stirring, until lightly browned.

❷ Add the chilli powder, tomatoes and stock, and cook until the tomatoes reduce to a sauce; mash the meat a little as it cooks.

❸ Add the chipotle chillies and continue to cook and mash until the sauce and meat are nearly blended.

❹ Serve the dish with a stack of warmed corn tortillas so that people can fill them with the meaty mixture to make tacos. Also serve soured cream, fresh coriander, radishes and lettuce for each person to add to the meat.

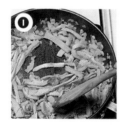

Fish

Many Mexican fish recipes include chillies, garlic and coriander, a trio of ingedients usually given extra zest with the juice of a lime. Several dishes in this section are based on this delicious combination of flavours, all very quick and easy – Pan-fried Scallops Mexicana can be prepared and cooked in moments. By contrast, Squid simmered with Tomatoes, Olives & Capers is cooked with herbs and spices to a stewlike consistency. Fish with Yucatecan flavours is a dish from the Yucatecan people of the Yucatan. The fish is dressed with a paste of fruit juice mixed with spices, wrapped in banana leaves, and steamed.

Fish with Yucatecan flavours

INGREDIENTS

4 tbsp annatto seeds,
    soaked in water
    overnight
3 garlic cloves, chopped
    finely
1 tbsp mild chilli powder
1 tbsp paprika
1 tsp ground cumin
½ tsp dried oregano
2 tbsp beer or tequila
juice of 1 lime and
    l orange or 3 tbsp
    pineapple juice
2 tbsp olive oil
2 tbsp chopped fresh
    coriander
¼ tsp ground cinnamon
¼ tsp ground cloves
1 kg/2 lb 4 oz swordfish
    steaks
banana leaves, for
    wrapping (optional)
fresh coriander leaves,
    to garnish
orange wedges, to
    serve

❶ Drain the annatto, put them in a mortar and crush them to a paste with a pestle. Work in the garlic, chilli powder, paprika, cumin, oregano, beer or tequila, fruit juice, olive oil, fresh coriander, cinnamon and cloves.

❷ Smear the paste over the fish and marinate in the refrigerator for at least 3 hours or overnight.

❸ Wrap the fish steak in banana leaves, tying with string to make packages. Bring water to the boil in a steamer, then add the packages to the top part of the steamer and cook for about 15 minutes, or until the fish is cooked through.

❹ Alternatively, cook the fish without wrapping it in the banana leaves. To cook on the grill, enclose it in a hinged basket, or place it on a rack, and cook over the hot coals for 5–6 minutes on each side, or until cooked through. Alternatively, cook the fish under a preheated grill for 5–6 minutes on each side, or until cooked through.

❺ Garnish with coriander and serve with orange wedges to squeeze over the fish.

easy

serves 4

20 minutes,
plus 3 hours
to marinate

20–25 minutes

Prawns in French Bean Sauce

INGREDIENTS

3 onions, chopped
5 garlic cloves, chopped
2 tbsp vegetable oil
5–7 ripe tomatoes,
    diced
175–225 g/6–8 oz
    French beans, cut into
    5 cm/2 inch pieces
    and blanched in
    boiling water for 1
    minute
¼ tsp ground cumin
pinch of ground mixed
    spice
pinch of ground
    cinnamon
½–1 canned chipotle
    chilli in adobo
    marinade, with some
    of the marinade
2 cups fish stock or
    water mixed with a
    fish stock cube
1 lb raw prawns, peeled
fresh coriander sprigs
1 lime, cut into wedges

❶ Fry the onion and garlic in the oil lightly over a low heat for 5–10 minutes, or until softened. Add the tomatoes and cook for an additional 2 minutes.

❷ Add the French beans, cumin, mixed spice, cinnamon, the chipotle chilli and adobe marinade, and the fish stock. Bring to the boil, then reduce the heat and simmer for a few minutes to combine the flavours.

❸ Add the prawns and cook for 1–2 minutes only, then remove the pan from the heat and leave the prawns to steep in the hot liquid to finish cooking. They are cooked when they have turned bright pink.

❹ Serve immediately, garnished with the fresh coriander and accompanied by the lime wedges.

 very easy

 serves 4

 10 minutes

 25 minutes

Squid simmered with Tomatoes, Olives & Capers

INGREDIENTS

3 tbsp extra-virgin olive
  oil
900 g/2 lb cleaned
  squid, cut into rings
  and tentacles
1 onion, chopped
3 garlic cloves, chopped
400 g/14 oz canned
  chopped tomatoes
½–1 fresh mildish green
  chilli, deseeded and
  chopped
1 tbsp finely chopped
  fresh parsley
¼ tsp chopped fresh
  thyme
¼ tsp chopped fresh
  oregano
¼ tsp chopped fresh
  marjoram
large pinch of ground
  cinnamon
large pinch of ground
  mixed spice
large pinch of sugar
15–20 pimiento-stuffed
  green olives, sliced
1 tbsp capers
salt and pepper
1 tbsp chopped fresh
  coriander, to garnish

❶ Heat the oil in a pan and lightly fry the squid until it turns opaque. Season with salt and pepper and remove from the pan with a slotted spoon.

❷ Add the onion and garlic to the remaining oil in the pan and fry until softened. Stir in the tomatoes, chillies, herbs, cinnamon, mixed spice, sugar and olives. Cover and cook over a medium–low heat for 5–10 minutes, or until the mixture thickens slightly. Uncover the pan and cook for an additional 5 minutes to concentrate the flavours.

❸ Stir in the reserved squid and any of the juices that have gathered. Add the capers and heat through.

❹ Adjust the seasoning, then serve immediately, garnished with fresh coriander.

 very easy

 serves 4–6

 10 minutes

 30 minutes

Pan-fried Scallops Mexicana

INGREDIENTS

25 g/1 oz butter

2 tbsp extra-virgin olive oil

625 g/1 lb 6 oz scallops, shelled

4–5 spring onions, thinly sliced

3–4 garlic cloves, chopped finely

½ fresh green chilli, deseeded and chopped finely

2 tbsp finely chopped fresh coriander

juice of ½ lime

salt and pepper

lime wedges, to serve

❶ Heat half the butter and olive oil in a heavy-based frying pan until the butter foams, then add the scallops and cook quickly until they just turn opaque. Do not overcook. Remove from the pan with a slotted spoon and keep warm.

❷ Add the remaining butter and oil to the pan, then toss in the spring onions and garlic and cook over a medium heat until the spring onions wilt. Return the scallops to the pan.

❸ Remove the pan from the heat and add the chilli, coriander and lime juice. Season with salt and pepper and stir to mix well.

❹ Serve immediately with lime wedges to squeeze over the scallops.

 extremely easy

 serves 4

 10 minutes

 10 minutes

FISH

Spicy Grilled Salmon

INGREDIENTS

4 salmon steaks, about
175–225 g/6–8 oz
each
lime slices, to garnish

MARINADE
4 garlic cloves, chopped
finely
2 tbsp extra-virgin olive oil
pinch of ground mixed
spice
pinch of ground
cinnamon
juice of 2 limes
1–2 tsp marinade from
canned chipotle
chillies or bottled
chipotle to chilli salsa
¼ tsp ground cumin
pinch of sugar
salt and pepper

TO SERVE
tomato wedges
3 spring onions,
chopped chopped
shredded lettuce

❶ To make the marinade, finely chop the garlic and place in a bowl with the olive oil, allspice, cinnamon, lime juice, chipotle marinade, cumin and sugar. Add salt and pepper and stir to combine.

❷ Coat the salmon with the garlic mixture, then place in a nonmetallic dish. Leave to marinate for at least an hour or overnight in the refrigerator.

❸ Transfer to a grill pan and cook under a preheated grill for 3-4 minutes on each side. Alternatively, cook the salmon over hot coals on a grill until cooked through.

❹ To serve, mix the tomato wedges with the spring onions. Place the salmon on individual plates and arrange the tomato salad and shredded lettuce alongside. Garnish with lime slices and serve.

 extremely easy

 serves 4

 10 minutes,
plus 1 hour
to marinate

 8 minutes

Fish baked with Lime

INGREDIENTS

1 kg/2 lb 4 oz white fish
  fillets, such as bass,
  flounder or cod
1 lime, halved
3 tbsp extra-virgin olive
  oil
1 large onion, chopped
  finely
3 garlic cloves, chopped
  finely
2–3 pickled jalapeño
  chillies (see Cook's
  Tip), chopped
6–8 tbsp chopped fresh
  coriander
salt and pepper
lemon and lime wedges,
  to serve

 extremely easy

 serves 4

 10 minutes

 25 minutes

❶ Place the fish fillets in a bowl and sprinkle with salt and pepper. Squeeze the juice from the lime over the fish.

❷ Heat the olive oil in a frying pan. Add the onion and garlic and fry for about 2 minutes, stirring frequently, until softened. Remove from the heat.

❸ Place a third of the onion mixture and a little of the chillies and coriander in the bottom of a shallow baking dish or roasting tin. Arrange the fish on top. Top with the remaining onion mixture, chillies, and coriander.

❹ Bake in a preheated oven at 180°C/350°F/Gas Mark 4 for about 15–20 minutes, or until the fish has become slightly opaque and firm to the touch. Serve at once, with lemon and lime wedges to squeeze over the fish.

COOK'S TIP
Pickled jalapeños are sold as jalapeños en escabeche and are available from delicatessens.

Salads, Snacks & Side Dishes

Many Mexican snacks are based on refried beans. These are pinto or borlotti beans which are cooked and mashed and then refried with onions and seasonings. The classic recipe, on page 62, is aptly named Mexican Refried Beans 'with everything'. No Mexican feast is complete without salsas and sauces (or moles) to accompany the beans, and the following pages include recipes for Hot Mexican Salsas and Mole Poblano, which includes chocolate among its mix of ingredients.

Hot Mexican Salsas

INGREDIENTS

TROPICAL FRUIT SALSA
½ sweet ripe pineapple, peeled, cored and diced
1 mango or papaya, peeled, deseeded and diced
½–1 fresh green chilli, such as jalapeño or serrano, deseeded and chopped
½–1 fresh red chilli, such as jalapeño or serrano, chopped
½ red onion, chopped
1 tbsp sugar
juice of 1 lime
3 tbsp chopped fresh mint
salt

SCORCHED CHILLI SALSA
1 green pepper
2–3 fresh green chillies, such as jalapeño or serrano
2 garlic cloves, chopped finely
juice of ½ lime
1 tsp salt
large pinch of dried oregano
large pinch of ground cumin
2–3 tbsp extra-virgin olive oil or vegetable oil

SALSA VERDE
1 lb fresh tomatillos, husks removed, cooked in a small amount of water until just tender, then chopped
1–2 green chillies, such as jalapeño or serrano, deseeded and chopped finely
1 green pepper or large mild green chilli, such as anaheim or poblano, deseeded and chopped
1 small onion, chopped
1 bunch fresh coriander leaves, chopped finely
½ tsp ground cumin
salt

❶ To make the tropical fruit salsa, combine all the ingredients in a large bowl, adding salt to taste. Cover the bowl and chill in the refrigerator until required.

❷ For scorched chilli salsa, char the chillies and pepper in an ungreased frying pan. Cool, deseed, skin and chop. Mix with the garlic, lime juice, salt and oil. Top with oregano and cumin.

❸ For salsa verde, combine the ingredients in a bowl, adding salt to taste. If a smoother sauce is preferred, blend the ingredients in a food processor. Spoon into a bowl to serve.

very easy

serves 4–6

20 minutes

15–20 minutes

Refried Bean Nachos

INGREDIENTS

400 g/14 oz refried
  beans
400 g/14 oz canned
  pinto beans, drained
large pinch of ground
  cumin
large pinch of mild chilli
  powder
175 g/6 oz tortilla chips
2 cups grated cheese,
  such as Cheddar
salsa of your choice
1 avocado, pitted, diced
  and tossed with lime
  juice
½ small onion or
  3–5 spring onions,
  chopped
2 ripe tomatoes, diced
handful of shredded
  lettuce
3–4 tbsp chopped fresh
  coriander
soured cream, to serve

❶ Place the refried beans in a pan with the pinto beans, cumin and chilli powder. Add enough water to make a thick souplike consistency, stirring gently so that the beans do not lose their texture.

❷ Heat the bean mixture over a medium heat until hot, then reduce the heat and keep warm while you prepare the rest of the dish.

❸ Arrange half the tortilla chips in a flameproof casserole or gratin dish and cover with the bean mixture. Sprinkle with the cheese and bake in a preheated oven at 200°C/400°F/Gas Mark 6 until the cheese melts. Alternatively, place the casserole under the grill and grill for 5–7 minutes, or until the cheese melts and lightly sizzles in places.

❹ Arrange on top of the melted cheese the salsa, avocado, onion, tomato, lettuce and fresh coriander. Surround with the remaining tortilla chips and serve immediately, accompanied by soured cream.

 extremely easy

 serves 4

 10 minutes

20–25 minutes

Tortas

4 crusty rolls, such as
   French rolls or
   bocadillos
melted butter or olive
   oil, for brushing
225 g/8 oz refried beans
350 g/12 oz each of
   shredded cooked
   chicken, browned
   chorizo pieces, sliced
   ham and cheese, or
   any leftover cooked
   meat you have to
   hand
1 ripe tomato, sliced or
   diced
1 small onion, chopped
   finely
2 tbsp chopped fresh
   coriander
1 avocado, stoned,
   sliced and tossed
   with lime juice
4–6 tbsp soured cream
salsa of your choice
handful of shredded
   lettuce

❶ Cut the rolls in half and remove a little of the crumb to make space for the filling.

❷ Brush the outside and inside of the rolls with butter or oil and toast, on both sides, on a hot griddle or frying pan for a few minutes until crisp. Alternatively, place in a preheated oven at 200°C/400°F/Gas Mark 6 until lightly toasted.

❸ Meanwhile, place the beans in a pan with a tiny amount of water and heat through gently.

❹ When the rolls are heated, spread one half of each roll generously with the beans, then top with a layer of cooked meat. Top with tomato, onion, fresh coriander and avocado.

❺ Spread soured cream thickly on the other side of each roll. Drizzle the salsa over the filling, add a little shredded lettuce, then sandwich the two sides of each roll together, pressing tightly. Serve immediately.

 very easy

 serves 4

 10 minutes

 5–10 minutes

Papaya, Avocado & Red Pepper Salad

INGREDIENTS

200 g/7 oz mixed green salad leaves
2–3 spring onions, chopped
3–4 tbsp chopped fresh coriander
1 small papaya
2 red peppers
1 avocado
1 tbsp lime juice
3–4 tbsp pumpkin seeds, preferably toasted (optional)

DRESSING
juice of 1 lime
large pinch of paprika,
large pinch of ground cumin
large pinch of sugar
1 garlic clove, chopped finely
4 tbsp extra-virgin olive oil
dash of white wine vinegar (optional)
salt

❶ Combine the salad leaves with the spring onions and coriander. Transfer to a serving dish.

❷ Cut the papaya in half and scoop out the seeds with a spoon. Cut into quarters, then remove the peel and slice the flesh. Arrange on top of the salad leaves. Cut the peppers in half and remove the cores and seeds, then slice thinly. Add to the salad leaves.

❸ Cut the avocado in half around the stone. Twist apart, then remove the pit with a knife. Carefully peel off the skin, dice the flesh and toss in lime juice to prevent discoloration. Add to the other salad ingredients.

❹ To make the dressing, whisk together the lime juice, paprika, ground cumin, sugar, garlic and olive oil. Add salt to taste.

❺ Pour the dressing over the salad and toss lightly, adding a dash of wine vinegar for a more intense flavour. Sprinkle with the toasted pumpkin seeds, if using.

 very easy

 serves 4

 15 minutes

 0 minutes

French Bean Salad with Feta Cheese

350 g/12 oz French beans, topped and tailed
1 red onion, chopped
3–4 tbsp chopped fresh coriander
2 radishes, sliced thinly
75 g/2³/₄ oz feta cheese, crumbled
1 tsp chopped fresh oregano or ¹/₂ tsp dried
2 tbsp red wine or fruit vinegar
100 ml/3¹/₂ fl oz extra-virgin olive oil
3 ripe tomatoes, cut into wedges
pepper

❶ Bring about 5 cm/2 inches water to the boil in the bottom of a steamer. Add the beans to the top part of the steamer, then cover and steam for about 5 minutes, or until just tender.

❷ Put the beans in a bowl and add the onion, coriander, radishes and feta cheese.

❸ Sprinkle the oregano over the salad, then grind pepper over to taste. Mix the vinegar and olive oil together and pour over the salad. Toss gently to mix well.

❹ Transfer to a serving platter and surround with the tomato wedges. Serve at once, or chill until ready to serve.

 extremely easy

 serves 4

 10 minutes

 5 minutes

Mole Poblano

INGREDIENTS

3 fresh mulato chillies
3 fresh mild ancho
    chillies
5 or 6 fresh anaheim
    chillies
1 onion, chopped
5 garlic cloves, chopped
450 g/1 lb ripe tomatoes
2 tortillas, preferably
    stale, cut into small
    pieces
pinch of cloves
pinch of fennel seeds
⅛ tsp each ground
    cinnamon, coriander,
    and cumin
3 tbsp lightly toasted
    sesame seeds or
    tahini
3 tbsp flaked or coarsely
    ground blanched
    almonds
2 tbsp raisins
1 tbsp peanut butter
    (optional)
500 ml/18 fl oz chicken
    stock
3–4 tbsp grated plain
    chocolate
2 tbsp mild chilli powder
3 tbsp vegetable oil
about 1 tbsp lime juice
salt and black pepper

❶ Using metal tongs, toast each chilli over an open flame for a few seconds until the colour darkens. Alternatively, roast in an ungreased frying pan over a medium heat, turning constantly, for about 30 seconds.

❷ Place the toasted chillies in a bowl or a pan and pour boiling water over to cover them. Put a lid on the pan and leave the chillies to soften for at least one hour, but preferably overnight. Once or twice, lift the lid and rearrange the chillies so that they soak evenly.

❸ Remove the chillies with a slotted spoon. Discard the stems and seeds, chop the flesh, and put it in a blender.

❹ Add the onion, garlic, tomatoes, tortillas, cloves, fennel seeds, cinnamon, coriander, cumin, sesame seeds, almonds, raisins and peanut butter (if using), then process to combine. With the motor running, add enough stock through the feed tube to make a smooth paste. Stir in the remaining stock, chocolate and chilli powder.

❺ Heat the oil in a pan until it is smoking, then pour in the mole mixture. It will sputter and pop as it hits the oil. Cook for 10 minutes, stirring occasionally to prevent burning. Season with salt, pepper and lime juice, then serve.

 easy

 serves 4

 10 minutes,
plus 1 hour
to soften

 15 minutes

Broccoli Enchiladas in Mild Chilli Sauce

INGREDIENTS

450 g/1 lb broccoli florets
225 g/8 oz ricotta cheese
1 garlic clove, chopped
½ tsp ground cumin
175–225 g/6–8 oz Cheddar cheese, grated
6–8 tbsp freshly grated Parmesan cheese
1 egg, beatenlightly
4–6 flour tortillas
vegetable oil, for greasing
mild red chilli sauce
1 cup chicken or vegetable stock
½ onion, chopped finely
3–4 tbsp chopped fresh coriander
3 ripe tomatoes, diced
salt and pepper
hot salsa, to serve

❶ Bring a pan of salted water to the boil. Add the broccoli, then bring back to the boil and blanch for 1 minute. Drain, refresh under cold running water, then drain again. Cut off the stems, peel and chop. Dice the broccoli heads.

❷ Mix the broccoli in a bowl with the ricotta cheese, garlic, cumin, half the Cheddar and half the Parmesan. Mix in the egg, and season.

❸ Heat the tortillas in a lightly greased non-stick frying pan, then fill each one with the broccoli mixture, and roll it up.

❹ Arrange the tortilla rolls in an ovenproof dish large enough to hold them in a single layer, then pour the mild chilli sauce over the top. Pour the stock over the tortillas.

❺ Top with the remaining Cheddar and Parmesan cheeses and bake in a preheated oven at 190 °C/375°F/Gas Mark 5 for about 30 minutes. Serve sprinkled with the onion, fresh coriander and tomatoes. Serve with a hot salsa.

 very easy

 serves 4

 15 minutes

 40 minutes

Mexican Refried Beans 'with everything'

INGREDIENTS

1–2 tbsp vegetable oil
1–1½ large onions,
    chopped
125 g/4½ oz bacon cut
    into small pieces
3–4 garlic cloves,
    chopped finely
about 1 tsp ground
    cumin
½ tsp mild chilli powder
400 g/14 oz canned
    tomatoes, diced and
    drained, reserving
    about 150–250 ml/
    5–9 fl oz of the juice
400 g/14 oz refried beans,
    broken up into pieces
scant ½ cup beer
400 g/14 oz canned
    pinto beans, drained
salt and pepper

TO SERVE
warmed flour tortillas
soured cream
sliced pickled chillies

 very easy

 serves 4

 10 minutes

 20 minutes

❶ Heat the oil in a frying pan. Add the onion and bacon and fry for about 5 minutes, or until they are just turning brown. Stir in the garlic, cumin and chilli powder, and continue to cook for 1 minute. Add the tomatoes and cook over a medium-high heat until the liquid has evaporated.

❷ Add the refried beans and mash lightly in the pan with the tomato mixture, adding beer as needed to thin out the beans and make them smoother. Lower the heat and cook, stirring, until the mixture is smooth and creamy.

❸ Add the pinto beans and stir well to combine. If the mixture is too thick, add a little of the reserved tomato juice. Adjust the spicing to taste. Season with salt and pepper and serve with warmed tortillas, soured cream and sliced chillies.

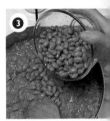

COOK'S TIP
The length of time the beans take to cook will depend on their age – old beans take longer than younger beans.

Spicy Fragrant Black Bean Chilli

INGREDIENTS

400 g/14 oz dried black
  beans
2 tbsp olive oil
1 onion, chopped
5 garlic cloves, chopped
  coarsely
2 slices bacon, diced
½–1 tsp ground cumin
½–1 tsp mild red chilli
  powder
1 red pepper, diced
1 carrot, diced
400 g/14 oz fresh
  tomatoes, diced; or
  chopped canned
1 bunch fresh coriander,
  roughly chopped
salt and pepper

 very easy

 serves 4

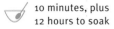 10 minutes, plus
12 hours to soak

2 hours,
45 minutes

❶ Soak the beans overnight, then drain. Put in a pan, then cover with water and bring to the boil. Boil for 10 minutes, then reduce the heat and simmer for about 1½ hours, or until tender. Drain well, reserving 250 ml/9 fl oz of the cooking liquid.

❷ Heat the oil in a frying pan. Add the onion and garlic, and fry for 2 minutes, stirring. Stir in the bacon (if using) and cook, stirring occasionally, until the bacon is cooked and the onions are softened.

❸ Stir in the cumin and red chilli powder and continue to cook for a moment or two. Add the red pepper, carrot, and tomatoes. Cook over a medium heat for about 5 minutes.

❹ Add half the coriander and the beans and their reserved liquid. Season with salt and pepper. Simmer for 30–45 minutes, or until thickened.

❺ Stir in the remaining coriander, adjust the seasoning, and serve the chilli at once.

COOK'S TIP
You can use canned beans in this recipe: drain them and use 250 ml/9 fl oz water for the liquid in Step 4.

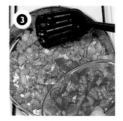

Rice with Lime

2 tbsp vegetable oil
1 small onion, chopped
   finely
3 garlic cloves, chopped
   finely
175 g/6 oz mixed long-
   grain and wild rice
2 cups chicken or
   vegetable stock
juice of 1 lime
1 tbsp chopped fresh
   coriander

❶ Heat the oil in a heavy-based pan or a flameproof casserole. Add the onion and garlic, and cook gently, stirring occasionally, for 2 minutes. Add the rice and cook for another minute, stirring. Pour in the stock, increase the heat, and bring the rice to a boil, then reduce the heat to a very low simmer.

❷ Cover and cook the rice for about 10 minutes, or until the rice is just tender and the liquid is absorbed.

❸ Sprinkle in the lime juice and fork the rice to fluff up and to mix the juice in. Sprinkle with the coriander and serve.

extremely easy

serves 4

5 minutes

20 minutes

COOK'S TIP
Garnish the rice with sautéed plantains: slice a ripe peeled plantain, preferably on the diagonal, then fry in a heavy-based pan in a small amount of oil until they have browned in spots and are tender. Arrange in the bowl of rice.

Eggs Oaxaca style

INGREDIENTS

1 kg/2 lb 4 oz ripe
   tomatoes
about 12 small button
   onions, halved
8 garlic cloves, whole
   and unpeeled
2 fresh mild green
   chillies
pinch of ground cumin
pinch of dried oregano,
pinch of sugar, if
   needed
2–3 tsp vegetable oil
8 eggs, beaten lightly
1–2 tbsp tomato purée
salt and pepper
1–2 tbsp chopped fresh
   coriander, to garnish

❶ Heat an ungreased frying pan, then add the tomatoes and char lightly, turning them once or twice. Allow to cool.

❷ Meanwhile, char the onions, garlic and chillies lightly in the frying pan. Allow to cool slightly.

❸ Cut the cooled tomatoes into pieces and place in a blender or a food processor, with their charred skins. Remove the stems and seeds from the chillies, then peel and chop them. Remove the skins from the garlic and chop them. Chop the onions roughly. Add the chillies, garlic, and onions to the tomatoes.

❹ Process to make a rough purée, then add the cumin and oregano. Season with salt and pepper to taste, and add sugar if needed.

❺ Heat the oil in a heavy-based frying pan, then add a ladleful of egg and cook to make a thin omelette. Continue to make omelettes, stacking them on a plate as they are cooked. Slice them into ribbons.

❻ Bring the sauce to a boil, then adjust the seasoning, adding tomato purée to taste. Add the omelette strips and warm them through, then serve at once, garnished with a sprinkling of fresh coriander.

 very easy

 serves 4

🥄 15 minutes

🕐 25–30 minutes

Desserts

If your sizzling, spicy-hot Mexican meal has left you feeling that your mouth is on fire, the idea of a dessert called Icy Fruit Blizzard will probably be very appealing. Mexican Chocolate Meringues, served with strawberries, chocolate-flavoured cream, and a sprinkling of cinnamon, round off a spicy dinner lightly and deliciously. The recipes in this part of the book are exotic compositions, with names to match. Aztec Oranges, for example, combines oranges, limes, and Tequila, and empanadas are pastries with a filling of bananas and chocolate.

Aztec Oranges

6 oranges
1 lime
2 tbsp tequila
*2 tbsp orange-flavoured
    liqueur*
*dark soft brown sugar,
    to taste*
*fine lime rind strips, to
    decorate
    (see Cook's Tip)*

❶ Using a sharp knife, cut a slice off the top and bottom of the oranges, then remove the peel and pith, cutting downward and taking care to retain the shape of the fruit.

❷ Holding each oranges on its side, cut it horizontally into slices of even thickness.

❸ Place the oranges in a bowl. Cut the lime in half and squeeze the juice over the oranges. Sprinkle with the tequila and liqueur, then sprinkle sugar over the top.

❹ Chill until ready to serve, then transfer to a serving dish and garnish with lime strips.

 extremely easy

 serves 4

 10 minutes, plus 1 hour to chill

 0 minutes

COOK'S TIP
To make the decoration, pare the rind from a lime finely using a vegetable peeler, then cut into thin strips. Add to boiling water and then blanch for 2 minutes. Drain in a sieve and rinse under cold running water. Drain again and pat dry with kitchen paper.

Pineapple Compôte with Tequila & Mint

INGREDIENTS

1 ripe pineapple
sugar, to taste
juice of 1 lemon
2–3 tbsp tequila or a
few drops of vanilla
essence
several sprigs of fresh
mint, leaves removed
and cut into thin
strips
fresh mint sprig, to
decorate

❶ Using a sharp knife, cut off the top and bottom of the pineapple. Place upright on a board, then slice off the skin, cutting downward. Cut in half, remove the core if desired, then cut the flesh into slices and the slices into chunks.

❷ Put the pineapple in a bowl and sprinkle with the sugar, lemon juice and tequila or vanilla essence.

❸ Toss the pineapple to coat the chunks well, then chill until ready to serve.

❹ To serve, arrange on a serving plate and sprinkle with the mint strips. Decorate with a mint sprig.

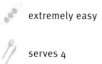 extremely easy

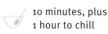 serves 4

10 minutes, plus 1 hour to chill

0 minutes

COOK'S TIP
Be careful to slice off the 'eyes' when removing the skin from the pineapple.

Icy Fruit Blizzard

INGREDIENTS

1 pineapple
1 large piece water
  melon, deseeded,
  peeled and cut into
  small pieces
225 g/8 oz strawberries
  or other berries, hulled
  and whole or sliced
1 mango, peach or
  nectarine, peeled and
  sliced
1 banana, peeled and
  sliced
orange juice
sugar, to taste

 extremely easy

 serves 4

20 minutes, plus
2 hours to chill

0 minutes

❶ Cover 2 baking sheets with a sheet of clingfilm. Arrange the fruit on top, and freeze for at least 2 hours, or until firm and icy.

❷ Place one type of fruit in a food processor and process until it is broken up into small pieces.

❸ Add a little orange juice and sugar to taste, and continue to process until it forms a granular mixture. Repeat with the remaining fruit. Arrange in chilled bowls and serve immediately.

COOK'S TIP
The fruit can be processed all together, if preferred, or use just one type of fruit – match the juice to the fruit.

Empanadas of Banana and Chocolate

about 8 sheets of filo
pastry, cut in half
lengthways
melted butter or
vegetable oil, for
brushing
2 ripe sweet bananas
1–2 tsp sugar
juice of ¼ lemon
175-200 g/6–7 oz plain
chocolate, broken
into small pieces
icing sugar, for dusting
ground cinnamon, for
dusting

 very easy

 serves 4

 15 minutes

15 minutes

COOK'S TIP
Use ready-made puff
pastry instead of filo
pastry to achieve a
more fluffy effect.

❶ Working one at a time, lay a long rectangular sheet of filo pastry in front of you and brush it with butter or oil.

❷ Peel and dice the bananas and place them in a bowl. Add the sugar and lemon juice, and stir well to combine. Stir in the chocolate.

❸ Place a couple of teaspoons of the banana and chocolate mixture in one corner of the pastry, then fold over into a triangle shape to enclose the filling. Continue to fold in a triangular shape, until the filo pastry is completely wrapped around the filling.

❹ Dust with icing sugar and cinnamon. Place on a baking sheet and continue the process with the remaining pastry and filling.

❺ Bake in a preheated oven at 190°C/375°F/Gas Mark 5 for about 15 minutes, or until the little pastries are golden. Remove from the oven and serve hot, warning your guests that the filling is very hot.

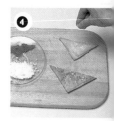

Torta del Cielo

INGREDIENTS

175 g/6 oz raw almonds,
   in their skins
2 sticks unsalted butter,
   at room temperature
200 g/7 oz sugar
3 eggs, beaten lightly
1 tsp almond essence
1 tsp vanilla essence
9 tbsp plain flour
a pinch of salt
butter, for greasing

TO SERVE
icing sugar, for dusting
flaked almonds, toasted

❶ Butter a 20 cm/8 inch round or square cake tin lightly, and line it with baking paper.

❷ Put the almonds in a food processor to form a crumbly mixture. Set aside.

❸ Beat the butter and sugar in a bowl until they form a smooth, fluffy mixture. Beat in the eggs, almonds, and almond and vanilla essences until well blended.

❹ Stir in the flour and salt and mix briefly until the flour is just incorporated.

❺ Pour or spoon the batter into the greased tin and smooth the surface. Bake in a preheated oven at 180°C/350°F/Gas Mark 4 for 40–50 minutes, or until the cake feels spongy when gently pressed.

❻ Remove from the oven and leave to cool on a wire rack. To serve, dust with icing sugar and decorate with toasted almonds.

 very easy

 serves 4

 15 minutes

 40–50 minutes,
plus cooling time

Mexican Chocolate Meringues

 very easy

 serves 4

 10 minutes

 3 hours

COOK'S TIP
To make the flavoured
cream, simply stir half-
melted chocolate
pieces into stiffly
whipped cream, then
chill until solid.

❶ Whisk the egg whites until they are foamy, then add the salt and cream of tartar and beat until very stiff. Whisk in the vanilla, then slowly whisk in the sugar, a small amount at a time, until the meringue is shiny and stiff. This should take about 3 minutes by hand, and less than a minute with an electric beater.

❷ Whisk in the cinnamon and grated chocolate. Spoon mounds of about 2 tablespoonfuls onto an ungreased, nonstick baking sheet. Space the mounds well.

❸ Place in a preheated oven at 150°C/300°F/Gas Mark 2 and cook for 3 hours, or until set.

❹ Carefully remove from the baking sheet. If the meringues are too moist and soft, return them to the oven to firm up and dry out more. Allow to cool completely.

❺ Before serving the meringues, dust them with cinnamon and accompany them with strawberries and chocolate-flavoured cream.

INDEX